A long time ago, as a little girl,
I dreamed of traveling all over the world,
And often I'd ask about the past
Driving everyone crazy fast!
Amused by this my parents thought,
Why not call me "History" for short?

Little Miss HISTORY Travels to
The NORTH POLE
© 2018 Barbara Ann Mojica. All Rights Reserved.

Published by eugenus STUDIOS, LLC
in The UNITED STATES of AMERICA

P.O. BOX 213
Valatie, NY 12184
E-Mail: Barbara@LittleMissHistory.com
WebSite: www.LittleMissHISTORY.com

ISBN-13: 978-0-9989154-2-5

No part of this book is to be reproduced or distributed in any format without the written permission of the author.

Dedicated to all those young and old who believe.

BARBARA ANN MOJICA'S
Little Miss HISTORY
Travels to
The NORTH POLE

Illustrations by VICTOR RAMON MOJICA

The North Pole is the most northern place on Earth. All longitude lines meet at the North Pole and go south in all directions, so there is no time zone here.

The North Pole sits on a floating ice sheet in the Arctic Ocean. No land lies beneath the ice.

Sunrise and sunset come once a year. The North Pole receives six months of daylight and six months of darkness. The Arctic's warmest month is July when temperatures hover below 10 degrees Celsius or 50 degrees Fahrenheit.

The Arctic Circle is an imaginary line around the Earth that forms the Arctic's boundary. Few animals live in this tundra, a frozen, treeless environment.

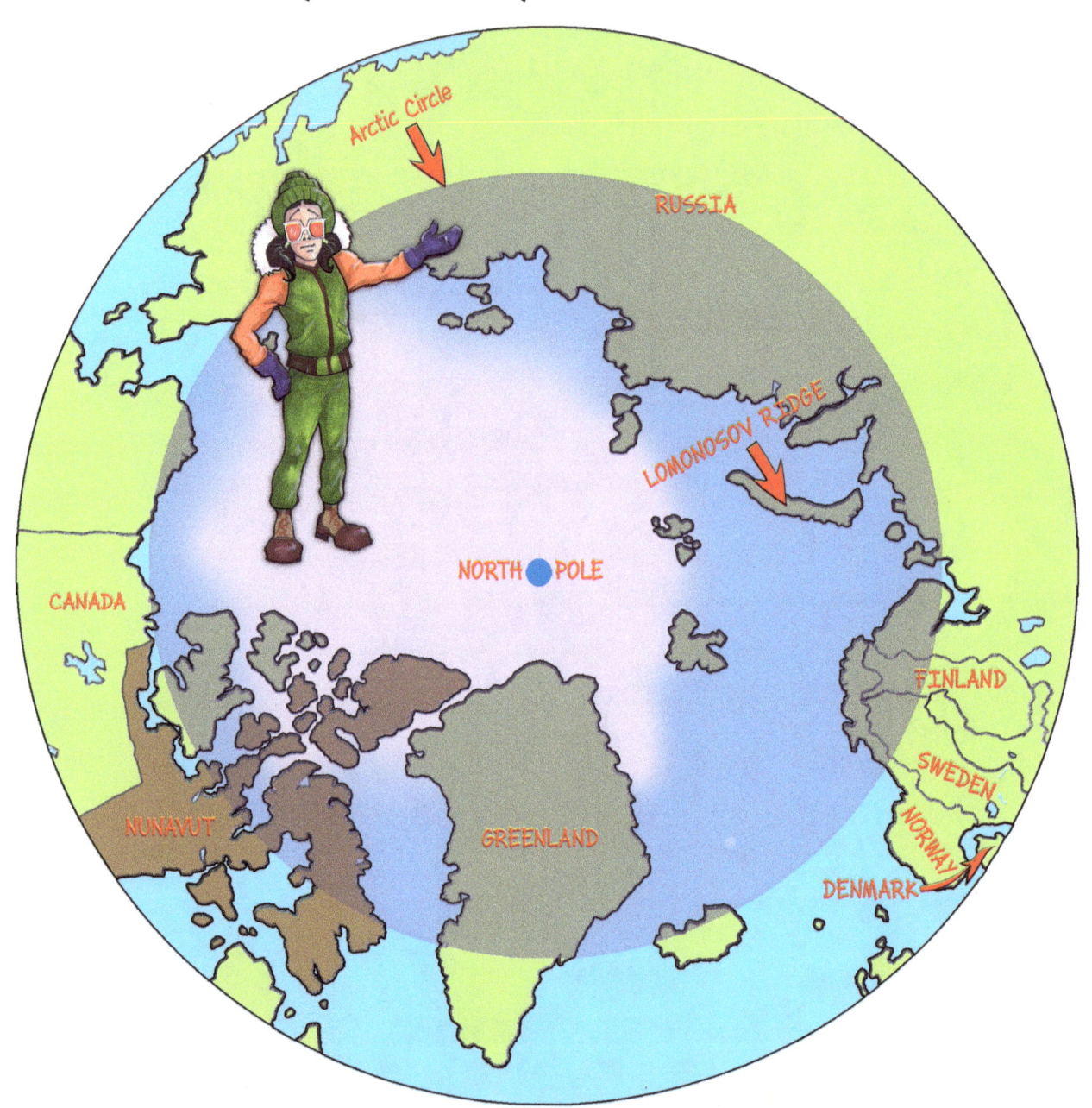

The closest lands to the Pole are Nunavut belonging to Canada and Greenland belonging to Denmark.

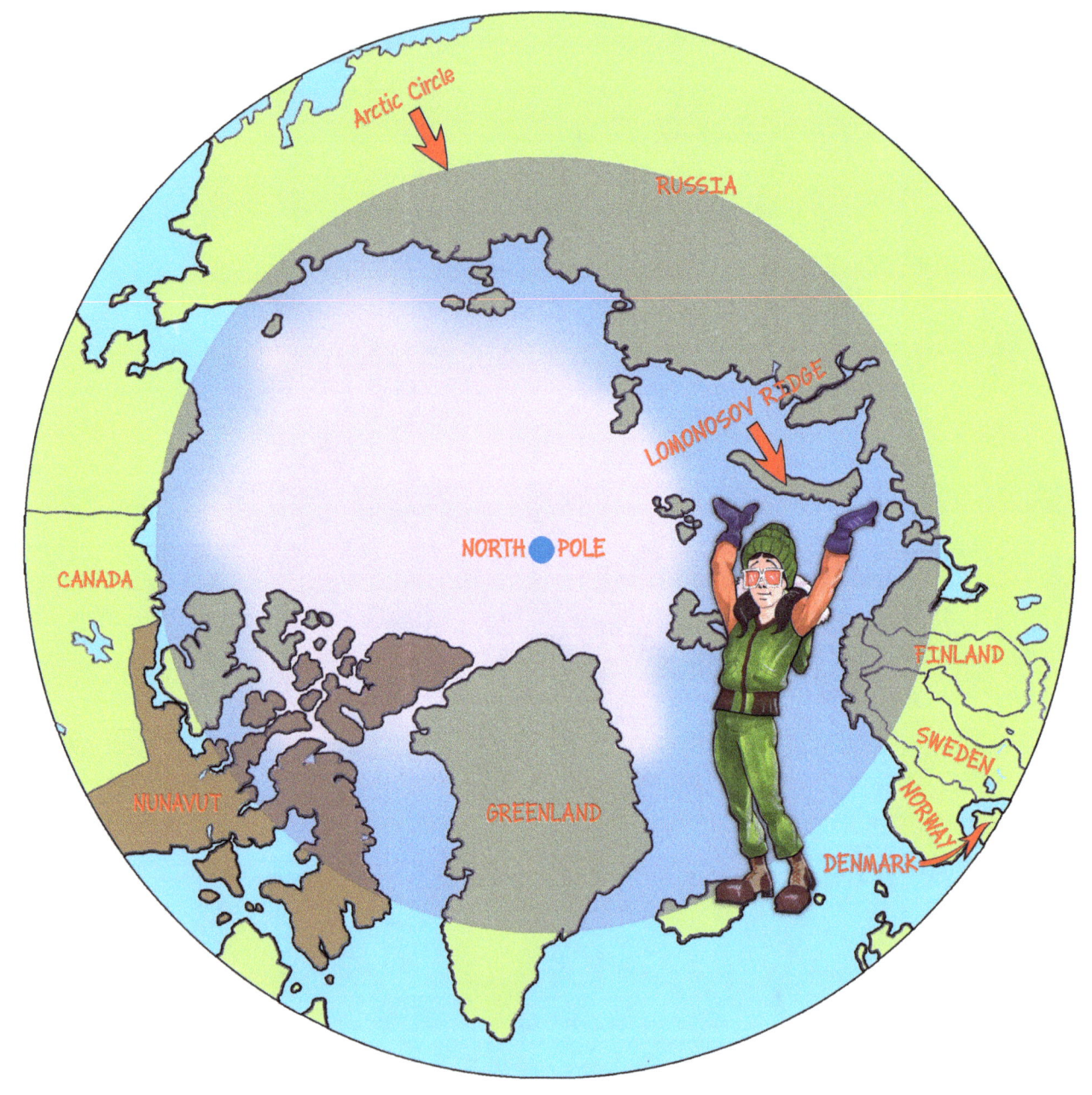

Russia and Denmark claim the Lomonosov Ridge. These mountains contain coal and gas underground.

Today most Inuit live in modern houses in Northern Canada, Alaska, Greenland, and Denmark.

Who is the real Santa Claus? Santa's story and his image changed over time. He owns many names: Santa Claus, Saint Nicholas, Saint Nick, Father Christmas, Kris Kringle, and Sinterklaas ...

... but all stories tell of a Santa bringing gifts to children sometime between December 6th and January 6th.

Ancient legends tell of the Scandinavian god named Odin who traveled on a wild hunt through the sky on a white horse with eight legs.

St. Nicholas was a real Christian bishop who lived in the fourth century in Myra, modern Turkey. He gave money to the poor.

In the 1930's American artists drew Santa Claus as a fat jolly man in a red suit with a long, white, beard to advertise Coca-Cola.

Our modern Santa Claus is a combination of all these figures. He has lots of helpers all over the world.

If Santa does live at the North Pole, where there is no time zone, then perhaps he can bring gifts to children all over the world.

That's all for now.
I'm off to my next adventure.
Until then

*"Happy Christmas to all,
and to all a good night."*

GLOSSARY
WORDS TO KNOW

ARCTIC OCEAN - the smallest and shallowest ocean. It surrounds the North Pole and is covered in ice for most of the year.

INDIGENOUS – original inhabitants of a region, natives.

INTERNATIONAL WATERS – places of the sea that are not under the control of any country.

INUIT – means "the people" One of the last native tribes to arrive in North America, often called Eskimos.

LONGITUDE LINES – imaginary up and down lines that run around the Earth and meet at the North and South Poles.

MAMMALS – animals that are warm-blooded with a backbone. They feed their young milk and have skin covered with hair or fur.

MIGRATORY BIRDS – birds that fly long, distances from season to season from one place to another and back again.

TIME ZONE – The local time of a region or country that is earlier or later than neighboring regions.

TRUDGE – walk slowly with heavy steps.

TUNDRA – a treeless environment where the soil is permanently frozen and where few animals live.

www.ingramcontent.com/pod-product-compliance
Lightning Source LLC
Chambersburg PA
CBHW061147010526
44118CB00026B/2904